You Are

TRUSTING GOD TO DEFINE WHO YOU ARE

Megan Wurzelbacher

This book is presented as a gift

To: _____

*By:*_____

*Date:*_____

You Are

Trusting God to define who you are

By: Megan Wurzelbacher

Published by: She Perseveres LLC

ISBN-10: 0692118209

ISBN-13: 978-0692118207

Library of Congress Control Number: 2018905353

Copyright © 2018 by She Perseveres LLC

She Perseveres LLC

megan@sheperseveres.com

www.sheperseveres.com

Printed in the United States of America

First Edition May 2018

This devotional is dedicated to my daughter, Kentlie Wurzelbacher. May you always trust God to define who you are. Remember you are a daughter of the King with a great purpose! I love you and I am so thankful God gave me my own little princess.

Love Always and Forever,

Mama

Contents

Connection

Join us as we are learning to trust God to define who we are!

Social Media

Let us know where you are in your journey upload the status for each chapter to your social media including the hashtags, add a picture if you would like!

Trusting God to define me! #youare #sheperseveres

Find us online:

http://www.sheperseveres.com/you-are/

Facebook:

https://www.facebook.com/sheperseveresllc/

Private Facebook Group: She Perseveres Group

https://www.facebook.com/groups/1726544080724161/

Instagram:

https://www.instagram.com/sheperseveres/

Pinterest:

https://www.pinterest.com/sheperseveres/pins/

Introduction

Introduction

Have you ever set out to find yourself? Have you ever wondered what your purpose was? Have you ever felt lost? Have you ever been confused about who you are? Have you ever needed to know who you are meant to be? Have you ever labeled yourself based on your experiences or others? Have you ever been ashamed of the labels you wear? I'm pretty sure if you can feel a heart beating in your chest that you answered yes to at least one of the above questions.

We all crave the sense of purpose and knowing who we are and what we were created for. We all are affected by our experiences and by others. We all are wearing labels of who we think we are.

As we go through our journey enduring various situations and interacting with people we begin to get to know ourselves in ways that have been impacted by others. We attach various labels to ourselves throughout our lives. Those labels are based on who we believe we are. We then begin to wear said labels as name tags every day of our lives.

Unfortunately, those name tags are filled with labels that are all too often negative. They may be based on who we see ourselves as, who others have told us we are, or what our past makes us believe we are. Such labels can be detrimental to how we feel about ourselves. These labels do not only affect our personal internal feelings but also how we present ourselves ultimately leading to how we live our lives.

You may have allowed the following to define who you are; the words of others, the actions of others, your accomplishments, your failures, your skills, your abilities, your disabilities, your childhood, your past, your relationships, your religion, your ethnicity, your faith, your culture, your race, your gender, your age, your career, your education, your family, your socioeconomic status, your appearance, and the list goes on. Be it negative or positive many factors and individuals take a large part in who we believe ourselves to be.

I, like so many others, let the things others said to me, about me, and the experiences I had deciphered who I believed I was at a young age. I felt inadequate, unpopular, unloved, alone, unworthy, and devalued.

Though no one had ever directly said I was inadequate I truly felt and believed that I was. I carried this label of "inadequate" for years based on my experiences, my conversations, my friendships, and my relationships. I continued to carry these inaccurate and untrue labels of who I was for many years. I allowed these labels to not only affect my self-perception but also the perception of who others viewed me.

Maybe the words your parents have said to you throughout your life have left you feeling unloved. Your boyfriend has made you feel unworthy not just through his words but also through his actions. You feel invisible every day at school, at work, at home and you just know that you bring no value to others. You feel alone because no one can relate to the struggles you face, and they would just never understand. You can never live up to the expectations you have set for your own education and career so why even try, you feel like a failure. We all struggle, we all feel less than, and we all wear these labels. We allow them to hold us back and carry them around like heavy chains. Preventing us from fulfilling our purposes, burdening us with hurtful emotions, and robbing us of any joy in our lives.

Instead of allowing these past experiences, people, and various other factors to define who we are we need to come to the realization that who we are can only be defined by our Creator.

Chapter One

Knowing

Who You Are

Knowing Who You Are

Though our experiences and others can influence who we are they should not fully define who we are. Not understanding who I was created to be impacted my life negatively from my childhood throughout my early adult years. I wish I would have known at an early age what it meant to know who you are through the eyes of our Creator.

There are numerous ideas and instructions telling us we need to find ourselves and figure out who we are. You commonly hear this idea of finding oneself during the college years. This is when you are also supposed to be discovering your abilities, skills, and desires for your future career. I was the high school student who was just happy to graduate. I did not have any real plans of what I wanted to do or who I was going to be.

Looking back now I realize I wasn't going to know who I was supposed to be or what I was supposed to do because I did not ask. I did not make decisions based on prayer and communication with God. I made decisions of who I was based on what other people told me, based on my past experiences, based on what my parents wanted me to do, based on how much money I would make, based on what my teacher thought I would be good at, and never based on what my Creator had actually created me to be. Sounds crazy to me now to think I was making such life-changing decisions about who I was and who I was going to be without even thinking to consult the one and only who already knew who I was.

Think about an inventor, when they create an invention they do not rely on others to define what that invention is. The inventor gives the invention its definition and its purpose because the inventor created it for a specific purpose. God is our inventor he created us for a specific purpose therefore, he is the one who defines who we are. We need to trust in God embracing who he has created us to be and who he says that we are.

"For we are God's handiwork, created in Jesus to do good works, which God prepared in advance for us to do." Ephesians 2:10 (NIV)

Knowing who you are requires that you confer with the only one who knows who you were, who you are, and who you are going to be. God is the only one who can define who you are. If you want access to that life-changing knowledge of who you are you must have a relationship with God. Having a relationship with God goes well above and beyond calling yourself a Christian and showing up to church on Sunday (or just on holidays). Sometimes going to church every time the door is open does not reflect on the status of your relationship with God either (I know this from personal experience).

Saying a prayer and telling others that you have asked Jesus into your heart does not always mean that you have a relationship with God. You need to have an authentic encounter with Jesus. You need to really get to know Him in a profound manner. Having a relationship with God is making a commitment to Him and to yourself. You have acknowledged your sin and asked for his forgiveness. You know he is the one and only true God. You believe his word to be true and relevant. You know he sent his son Jesus to die on the cross to forgive all our sins and to be raised from the dead three days later. You believe he is the Creator of all things. You submit yourself to his will and purposes for your life. Though it's not always easy you know and trust in Him. You have faith in Him. You have a desire to know Him more and more. You fear and respect Him. You live to tell others about Him. You love Him.

Relationships require work and communication. This is still true of the relationship you have with God. You must be willing to put forth an effort and be vulnerable in your relationship with Him. This is the most important relationship you will ever have and frequently the most difficult one. Being a Christian does not stop at saying a prayer or at being baptized. You must continue to build and grow in your relationship with God. You must be active in reading his Word, active in prayer communicating with Him daily, active in trusting Him, active in loving Him, active in loving others through Him, and active in a real thriving relationship with your Creator.

Sometimes we get so busy with life that we do not allow the focus to be on ourselves. As women, we are constantly pouring into others and their needs that we often put ourselves on the back burner so to speak. Most of the time this happens without us even realizing. This regrettably can mean that our relationship with God may not be prioritized. It is so important for us as women to be adamant about focusing on and prioritizing our relationship with God. We need to be filled with Him, so we can have something to pour back into others.

Not only does being filled with God allow us to pour into others and ourselves it also fills a natural void or vacancy that we all have. God created us to desire a deep and meaningful relationship with Him. When there is no meaningful relationship with Him we have an emptiness. When we have this vacancy in our hearts it allows insecurities and negative labels to creep right in and fill the space. Those insecurities can lead us down a dark path.

When you are not filled with your relationship you have with God you will begin to fill yourself with anything to try and make the emptiness go away. Maybe you have already been there and figured out how to fill this vacancy in your heart. Maybe you do not even realize that you are allowing your own insecurities to fill a vacancy only God can fill. It could be your relationships, your eating habits, your desire for financial success, or even your need to feel popular and included. No matter what your insecurities from these false labels lead to you can never fill the emptiness with your own desires and needs.

Maybe you already know who you are in Jesus and you are secure in that identity. Not only is that remarkable for you but it is also important for those around you. Use that wisdom to help others by sharing who God truly is and therefore helping them to understand who they can be through Him. Though you are already assured of who you are it is also just as important to be reminded of those truths.

The enemy is in battle with us daily to try everything he can to cause friction in our relationship with God. Using others, experiences, and sometimes even our own negative labels the enemy is always at work to try and destroy the relationship we have with God. You must stand firm against the lies of the enemy. You need that strong foundation with God, so you can be assured of who you are through Him regardless of the enemy's tactics.

Whether you are unsure of who God is, unsure of who you are, or you need to be reminded of either I am so glad you are here. Knowing who you truly are is life-changing knowledge. So regardless of what others have said to you, what they have said about you, what others have done to you, or what others have not done for you let's dig deeper, so you can know who you are because of whose you are.

Knowing Who You Are

Bible Reading

1 Corinthians 3:16   2 Corinthians 1:21-22

Reflection

What would your name tag say today? Write your
labels on the name tag below.

Hello My Name Is

Now, it is time to learn to trust God to define who
you are. Join me and let us erase those name tags and
fill them with new and truthful labels.

Chapter Two

You Are Included

You Are Included

Have you ever felt alone? Have you ever felt like no one could possibly understand what you have been going through or what you have been feeling? Do you ever feel like it is impossible to make friends that you share something in common with? Do you feel like your responsibilities at work, school, and/or home are keeping you from making true connections with other women who could help encourage you, empathize with, and just be there for you? If you answered yes to any of the above questions this chapter is for you!

As I mentioned in the previous chapter I struggled from a very young age of feeling as if I did not fit in and I felt left out. I felt this way for years even into my early adult years. I felt like I was not good enough, I was not popular enough, I was not pretty enough, I was not smart enough, and the list goes on. These feelings can make you feel lonely and unincluded. Even if you have friends you may start to push them away because you just know they have never struggled the way you have, and they simply will not understand you.

You could be in a season of life where you are struggling whether it be something small or something completely life-changing you may feel alone. Possibly you are in the best season of your life where things could not be better, but you still have this overwhelming feeling of loneliness. You could have thousands of followers and friends online and just as many in your life offline, but you still feel all alone and/or unincluded.

When we feel alone or unincluded it leaves you in a very vulnerable emotional state allowing the enemy easier access to our insecurities. That gives the enemy ample opportunity to trick us into believing more lies about ourselves. This is when those labels that shape who we believe we are become negative and detrimental to the view we have of ourselves. If we feel alone, unincluded, and like no one understands we often will retreat from relationships with others. If we are alone and we do not have others showing us encouragement and love it pushes us further into our own negative space and darkness. Therefore, it is so much easier for us to start to believe the enemy's lies about who we are. Once he has convinced us of those negative labels and that we are on our own he has succeeded in pushing us further from carrying out the purpose God has for us.

It is time to stop believing the enemy's lies. It is time for us to carry out the purpose that God has for our lives. God's desire for us is to live in community with others. He wants us to develop close friendships and relationships with others so that they can be there in our time of struggle. He wants us to have true friendships. He wants us to be able to learn from each other and hold each other accountable. He wants us to feel included and know we are not alone.

Our friendships are not to just be limited to what we think of in the traditional sense of friends. Our most important and deepest friendships may be with our family members and should most definitely include our spouse. In Song of Solomon, the Bride refers to her groom not only as her beloved but also as her friend.

Just like the relationship you have with your spouse a key component of any relationship is intimacy and any type of friendship is no different. Have you ever heard intimacy explained as "into-me-see"? Intimacy means to take the time to truly look into each other and get to know one another deeper than just surface level. Look beyond just common interests. Make the time to create deep friendships because they are a true investment.

In order to create true friendships, you must be vulnerable and honest with one another. I know for me personally being open to a new friendship can often be scary and difficult. Those labels that hold us back all to often prevent us from creating these meaningful friendships. We're too worried about what others think and how they will perceive us if we let them get to truly know us.

Ironically, once you are willing to show your true self to others they are less likely to create judgments about you and are more likely to feel comfortable enough to open up about themselves. Being your true-self allows you to have a real connection with others. This connection allows you to share more than just surface level information. Once you're able to connect on a deeper level with a new friend and get to know them you will realize you are not as alone in your feelings as you may have thought.

Making friends and opening up is even easier now than ever. Being able to connect online with others without having to see them face-to-face can sometimes make it easier to be open and honest even with your deepest struggles. Social media is a large part of our lives now and though it can be negative, social media has some amazing aspects as well. Using various social media outlets is a great way to create friendships and community that can help you feel included.

I know personally as a mom who homeschools and travels full time it can be really hard to find time for yourself. When you can't even find time for yourself it makes it that much harder to make a friendship with someone else. Writing this book, I hope to create a community of women who can find each other and relate to each other based on social media and share their stories. Feeling included, having other women to do life with, feeling understood, finding mentors, being encouraged, and being inspired is exactly what God wants for you.

Social media allows us to create friendships and allows us to feel included regardless of our locations, our availability, our careers, our schedules, or any social anxiety we may have. There are so many different groups on social media where every woman can relate and be included. Social media allows you to get to know the other people based on their post online and then decide if you feel comfortable enough to post yourself. You can post as much or as little as you want without feeling pressured to form a friendship right away. By simply joining a social media group of something that interest you or something that you've been through you will quickly see you're not alone.

While social media is an amazing tool for building friendships that would not be possible otherwise having friends, who are a part of your life and within a close physical location is highly important. Having friendships that include those who can come to you in times of need as well as in times of celebration is crucial. There is just something that cannot be denied about those friendships with others who can come to you for a face to face conversation and hug you through hard times or times of encouragement. Having a close friendship with other Christian women is vital not only for some girl time but for some amazing spiritual growth. As you build these deep relationships with your friends in the Christian community you build a force that can be powerful against the enemy and protect you against his strategies.

While our friendships with others are important we need to remember our most important and deepest friendship is to be with Jesus. Before we are able to build true and meaningful friendships with others we must also be mindful of who our most prioritized friendship should be with. An intimate and strong relationship with Jesus is what allows all other friendships to be true and meaningful.

Join me and the amazing community of women who are just like you and want to put Jesus first and be included! We can learn to continue trusting God to define who we are as we grow as friends in a community of Jesus loving women.

You Are Included

Bible Reading

Galatians 6:2 John 15:12-13

Reflection

What is your largest obstacle you face when creating intimate relationships?

Can you be more vulnerable to deepen your relationships (with God, spouse, and/or friends)?

Connection: Join our private Facebook group to develop new friendships with other women trusting God today!

Social Media Status: *You are included! I am included! #youare #sheperseveres*

Chapter Three

You Are Worthy

You Are Worthy

So many women feel unworthy or invaluable. When I think of being worthy I think of being important. Having worth also means that you're special or you have special qualities. If you're worthy it means you're deserving of special recognition.

We often look for our self-worth in the relationships we have with others. I know in my past I was more than guilty of looking for my worth in all the wrong places. I was a shy and socially awkward middle schooler. I never felt like I could keep up with the other girls in my class whether it be based on physical appearance, socially, or even based on the clothing they were all wearing. Sadly, I was so focused on outward appearance, social status, and attention from others that my self-esteem and self-worth were based on those things. This, unfortunately, followed me well beyond my middle school years.

I never shared my struggles or insecurities with anyone; friends, parents, not even with God. Though I now know he was always there I never once thought to ask God for help, guidance, or in any way did I think he was the answer for my issues. I really did not think that taking my feelings to God was even an option. Fast forward many years later and I'm married. My husband is truly a blessing to my life in many ways. He treats me with the utmost respect and reminds me that I am worthy, that I am valued, and that I am loved. However, through my insecurities and the enemy's lies in our marriage, those feelings of not being worthy crept back in and made an impact on my marriage.

After the birth of baby number three, I was struggling, in every aspect of the word. I was raising three kids, working outside the home, attending graduate school, unable to make ends meet, and unsure of what our future looked like. I was exhausted, overwhelmed, and felt as if I could not keep up. I was hating every aspect of my post-baby body and I was feeling physically touched out and overwhelmed from taking care of babies ages five and under. My husband was overworked at two separate jobs, remodeling our home, and completely exhausted. I felt a complete lack of intimacy in our relationship. I felt as if he just did not understand what I was going through. I felt like I was failing Him, our marriage, and our children. I felt like I was not worthy of anything.

During this time, I attended a woman's conference and I was inspired to spend time alone in my Bible. God spoke to me through this time and it finally clicked for me. I realized I was wrong, I am worthy. I was depending on my husband to meet all my needs and encourage me when I was feeling unworthy and inadequate. I was craving a sense of intimacy and attention that could never be fulfilled because that was not the source of my need.

I was worried about my physical appearance and my post-baby body. Looking back, I realized just a few years prior I was worried about my chances to become pregnant again in the first place and if I would be able to carry a healthy baby to full term following the miscarriage of our first child. I was feeling touched out from raising three little ones who were overwhelming me with their needs during a hectic time with my job and my education. However just a few years before I longed for the chance to just have one moment to touch the child I carried in my womb but never got to hold. I realized everything I had in my life at that moment was everything I had once prayed for. I realized I needed to give thanks for all I had and stop feeling like something was missing or like I was not worthy of what I already had. I also for the first time was able to understand that my needs can only be fulfilled fully by God and the relationship I have with Him. At this point in my life, he had already fulfilled so many of my needs, I was just too selfish to recognize it.

Our worth comes from God and his plan and purpose for us. We are worthy because God created us. The Word of God tells us that we were wonderfully created in the image of God. He created me to be the wife of my best friend. He created me to be the mother of these amazing small and often needy little gifts who truly give me such purpose. Really take the time to stop and think about this; if you are a mother, God created you knowing what kind of mommy your children needed and he chose you. God created you and arranged every step that led you to your spouse because he knew you were the wife that was needed. You are the daughter that was hand chosen by God to bless your parents in ways only you could.

God has created us each for a purpose. God's plan and purpose make us important. Everything about who he created us to be was done with the utmost intention. He sees us as an integral part of his greater plan. Not only does God see you as worthy he values every aspect of who you are. You are special with special God-given gifts. You are cherished by the Creator of this entire universe. You are valued and worth so much to God that not only does he have a special plan and purpose for your unique talents he also sent his one and only son to die for you. Think about that, God knew before you were even created that you are worthy enough for Jesus his one and only son to suffer and die for you. Who needs attention for outer appearance, a social status, a career, or from any certain person when God Himself has given so much attention just for you! Your value and your worth comes through God, not others, not clothes, not cars, not careers, not degrees, not any other material or worldly entity. You need to know God and have a true relationship with Him. If your relationship with God is strong he will be the foundation that your confidence, self-esteem, and self-love grow from.

You Are Worthy

Bible Reading

Genesis 1:27 Psalm 139:13-14

Reflection

Has someone made you feel unworthy? Was it their actions or their words?

What roles has God given you that shows you are worthy to Him?

Connection: Let the women in your life know they are worthy! Join us on Instagram and Facebook and tag your daughters, sisters, mothers, aunts, and friends online.

Social Media: *You are worthy! I am worthy! #youare #sheperseveres*

Chapter Four

You Are

Remembered

You Are Remembered

Sometimes when life gets hard it's easy to think God has forgotten about us. When plans don't work out or we're facing difficult times in our lives we wonder how God can let us suffer.

When life becomes too much to handle or tragedy strikes we may wonder if he even remembers we're here. Remembrance is not just a feeling it is an action. Actions of love show others they are remembered.

My life during my adolescence and early adulthood were difficult. I did not feel as if I was remembered by God during those years. My life was far from what God had planned for me. Though I had been saved and baptized at a young age I began to stray from my relationship with God. I thought that being saved was simply enough. I prayed the sinners' prayer, was told I had Jesus in my heart, and then I was baptized. I was a Christian and I was not going to hell so that was all I felt I needed.

However, I did not have an interactive relationship with God as a teenager. By the beginning of my junior year of high-school, I had few true friendships and many partying acquaintances. I had lied more times to my parents, family, friends, and even myself that I could have ever kept track of. I spent more nights drunk than sober. School was never a priority I just tried to make sure I would graduate. I have more than regret for the life-changing decisions I made as a teenager.

To add to my already low self-esteem and poor decision making the rumors that circled because of my decisions were even more damaging than the truth. I had been in situations that could have led to arrest, jail, physical harm, sexual abuse, rape, and even death. To say that I persevered by simply surviving my early teenage years is truly an understatement.

Just before my eighteenth birthday, I met Jason, my husband. Neither of us wanted to be in a relationship and from the very beginning we made that very clear to each other. We continued dating throughout my last year of high school though neither of us thought it would ever be a serious relationship.

As I entered my early twenties and college Jason and I were still dating. During this time, I was still living life on my terms and not on God's. We argued a lot at those early stages of our relationship. My opinion of myself, my past, and my insecurities all contributed to the negativity in our relationship.

In retrospect, it is also obvious the fact that I kept God at a distance and absolutely in no way was he a part of mine and Jason's relationship put us in a dark place as a couple. Over the next couple of years, Jason and I had gone through the ebb and flows of our relationship and eventually, we came to a turning point. We truly developed a new friendship that changed our relationship completely. We finally began to respect each other the way we should have done from the beginning but, we were still relying on ourselves with no true relationship with God. As our friendship and relationship began to grow we were very much in love with one another and ready to take the next step.

Shortly after getting married Jason and I decided we wanted to start our family. November 20, 2009, we found out we were going to have a baby and we were going to start building our family we had dreamed of. After spreading the amazing news to all our family and friends on Thanksgiving. New Year's Eve soon came, and I would remember this particular holiday for the rest of my life. I was almost fourteen weeks pregnant and my family and my husband's family enjoyed a great dinner. After dinner, I realized I was having some issues.

The next couple of days were unlike anything I had ever experienced. I called my doctor for a second time that weekend and I was instructed to go to the emergency room. After a horrendously long wait in the emergency room and many tests later the doctor started toward the door and my nerves set in, the look on his face said it all but I was still hopeful that was just me making things out to be worse than they were. There is no way to describe the next twenty minutes or so of this time in my life other than it felt like everything was in slow motion like I was dreaming.

The doctor put his head down and said he was sorry, but I had lost the baby and that's all I heard, and I broke down. I buried my face in my husband's chest as he embraced me with his arms I could hear Him and my parents' reaction of shock and sadness, but it was still like I was alone. I instantly felt empty both physically and emotionally, my heart was broken. I had a missed miscarriage, meaning the baby had died weeks before my body realized the pregnancy was over, so I was still growing bigger and still having pregnancy symptoms. January 5, 2010, I was scheduled for a D&C.

As the days passed after our loss I had a lot of time to reflect and think about my life. I had prayed more in that week than I really had ever before in my life. I was able to realize I needed to stop living my life for me and start living my life for God. He is in full control of my life and I need to remember that and live for his purposes. I also realized that without God and the relationship I rediscovered with Him I never would have made it through such a tragic event in my life. I believe that the hardships and tragedies we face in life are often the very things that God can use as a foundation to build our faith in Him.

As many who have lost a child will tell you the most important thing for us as parents is that our child is remembered. No matter how early in pregnancy or how old the child may have been as a mother it is the most important need, for the child to be remembered and not forgotten. Just like I so desire for my baby KW to be remembered I too want to be remembered. No one wants to feel like they have been forgotten.

I have learned that just like in other difficult times of my life and at the time of our loss, God had never forgotten me. Though I may have been distant from Him, he never left me, he never distanced Himself, he has always remembered me. He has remembered you. No matter how far from God you may be feeling, how forgotten you may feel, or how invisible you may feel, God remembers you and he has not forsaken you. In the book of Joshua, we are told that God will never leave us, he will never abandon us.

I can't help but think what my adolescence and early adulthood would have been like if I would have simply understood what having a relationship with God meant. Though he was not my priority, I know I was still his priority. I am so thankful for his unconditional love, grace, and protection that he extended to me during those difficult years, even though I was not reaching out to Him.

Maybe you also need to refresh your relationship with God. God has not forgotten you and you should not forget Him. Similarly, God remembered Noah, his family, and the animals on the Ark. Even during such a chaotic and devastating time he never forgot Noah or his family. God entered a promise with us through Noah and the placement of a rainbow in the sky. This everlasting promise shows us that God remembered Noah's faith and he would never allow another flood, to that extent, again. His promise was true in my life as the storm of pregnancy loss ended he blessed our family with a rainbow in the form of a precious baby boy just a few months later.

Simply trust in Him and call upon Him. God will always be there, he will always remember you. He will always extend his unconditional love, unending grace, and protection.

You are Remembered

Bible Reading

Isaiah 49:15 Genesis 8:1

Reflection

Think of a time God remembered you during a hard season of life. Did you seek Him at that time?

What action or step of obedience can you take to show God that you have remembered Him?

Connection

Let others know God has remembered them through your actions. Connect with someone through Social Media let them know you have remembered them and you are praying for them.

Social Media: *You are remembered! I am remembered! #youare #sheperseveres*

Chapter Five

You Are Loved

You Are Loved

Have you ever felt unloved? If we are all honest with ourselves we have all experienced this debilitating feeling. As humans, we were created to crave love so feeling unloved is nothing to be ashamed of. God created us to crave love, specifically his love. You may have the most loving family and the most fulfilling relationships regardless you still desperately need to feel loved. You could have also struggled throughout your life having never felt loved at all.

Feeling unloved may occur during everyday life and even then, it's such a difficult feeling to understand, own, and repair. However, during hardships and life's difficult seasons feeling unloved is especially damaging. When you are struggling emotionally, mentally, and/or physically the support you need most is unconditional love.

For me, one of the hardest seasons of my life was after the loss of our first child. I knew in order to just feel like I could survive the loss and get through the tragedy of a miscarriage I needed as much support and love that I could possibly get. I was beyond blessed for the love and support my husband and family gave me during the hardest stages of my grief. However, their love could not fulfill a deeper need I had for a divine unconditional love. The emptiness and the loneliness I felt following the miscarriage could only be healed through Jesus' unconditional love and I knew I needed to reach out to Him.

As I began to rekindle the relationships I had with God I experienced a sense of love I had been lacking and needing. Though I had love from those surrounding me the divine and perfect love from God was able to fulfill me in ways their love could not. For years I was searching for something to feel the void I felt in my life and until the loss of our Baby KW I did not know why. I soon realized the void I was feeling was love more specifically an unconditional, unchanging, and unending love. A divine love that could fulfill all my needs was the void.

I understood I had strayed from the relationship I once had with God. When I walked away from Him there was an emptiness left within me. When you have an emptiness where God's love is supposed to be that space becomes filled with hurt, fear, loneliness, self-doubt, and insecurities. I struggled all through my adolescence and early twenties with all those issues never realizing it was because the lack of relationship I had with God.

I knew God had never left me but instead, I had turned my back on Him. There was never a specific moment that it occurred it was just a culmination of events that pushed me further from Him. I hope by sharing this you too will realize that no matter what God will never leave you. God will never love you any less. No matter how far you may be from God he is still there. Your past or present mistakes or issues will not take God's love from you. Just always know that his unconditional love always remains.

God's love is the only love we ever need to fulfill us. When you feel unloved and like no one is meeting your needs it may be because you are not looking for love in the right place. You need a one of a kind divine love that is all fulfilling. This type of divine love is something only God can offer us.

His love is so amazing that not only is it unconditional and eternal it is a free gift. You do not need to earn God's love. We have not done anything to deserve God's divine love. There are no strings attached to his love. He just simply loves us unconditionally as a true and free gift to us.

God loved you before you were even created. He loved you before you could even earn love from anyone. God showed us the magnitude of his love for us when he sent his only son to die on the cross for our sins. Really let this sink in, think about this; God loves you so much that even before you were thought of by your parents, before you were created in your mother's womb, and before you were born he sent his one and only child to be tortured and be put to death so you could be forgiven of your sins and have eternal life with Him in Heaven. This is beyond any other sacrifice for love we could ever experience.

If you are lacking love from your parents God's love is more powerful than their love ever could have been in the first place. His love is more fulfilling in every way. If you are lacking love from a spouse or other type of relationship again God's love is more fulfilling than their love ever could have been in the first place. You can only find the type of love you need to fill wholly loved with God and no one else.

Do not fall for the enemy's tricks and believe that you are unlovable or unloved. You are more than loved with the perfect unconditional and divine love only God can give. God loves you and his love is more than all you need.

You Are Loved
Bible Reading
Romans 5:8 1 John 4:16

Reflection

Have you ever felt unloved? Who have you desired love from the most?

When do you feel God's love the most?

Connection: Join us in our private Facebook group and let us know how God has shown you love this past year. If you find yourself needing to be reminded that God loves you let us know that in our group, we are here to encourage each other.

Social Media: You are loved! I am loved! #youare #sheperseveres

Chapter Six

You are Significant

You Are Significant

If I could go back in time I would love to tell my eleven-year-old self, "You are SIGNIFICANT".

Because middle school crushed my confidence. I did not feel as if I fit in I was envious of others for their clothes, their hair, their makeup, their social life, and just never thought I was enough. I did not feel like I fit in. These feelings led to insecurities that shaped my behavior, my self-esteem, and who I believed I was. Had I just known and fully understood that I was (am) significant my entire adolescence and young adulthood would have been completely different. Less lonely, less insecure, less complicated, less hurtful, less dangerous, less regretful.

As women from a young age, we often allow ourselves to feel insignificant due to our insecurities and our comparisons. I would also like to tell my younger self that God created each one of us to be different, unique, special, and fitting perfectly into who HE wanted us to be.

God's perfect plan for who we are is so unique for each of us that we were never meant to be like others he made us each special, so we are incomparable. The plan that God has for you was designed especially for you and only you. You are significant enough to the Creator that he designed you with a special plan designed just for you.

Today with social media it is even harder not to get caught up in comparing ourselves with others. One important aspect to remember about social media is that everyone is only showing their highlight reel of life. In other words what you are seeing others display on social media is only what they choose to show you. They are showing you the best parts of their day, the best trips they take, the best dinners they eat, the best hair and makeup they have done, the best clothing they have. They are not sharing every aspect of their life and most definitely not their hardest times.

No one is posting a selfie with yesterday's eyeliner smeared across their face and their messy bun falling half off their head. No one is posting a video of their toddler throwing a tantrum while they are being yelled at by you to just go to bed for the last time. Everyone wants to show what they want others to perceive about their lives, they are not showing their real life. No matter what your perceived reality is, or your true reality is you are always significant to God and his plan. You do not have to be famous, wealthy, or successful in the definition of this world to be significant.

You were created for a special significant purpose by the Creator of all things. You have so many various roles to fulfill in your life. You were created for each of those roles. Your role as a daughter is significant. Your role as a wife is significant. Your role as a mother is significant. Your role as a sister, aunt, grandmother, cousin, teacher, lawyer, homeschool mother, stay at home mom, working mom, college student, high school student, are all significant. You are significant because your most important role is that as a daughter of the King.

Being a daughter of the King means you have fully submitted yourself in your relationship with God. You are making God your priority and continuing to pursue Him in an intimate connection. As your relationship with Him grows you will begin to become a reflection of who he is, and show his character through yours. Just as we inherit traits and attributes from our biological parents we also inherit traits and attributes of God. So, no matter how insignificant we may feel in various moments of our lives we know if our character is reflecting that of God we could never be insignificant, and we are a crucial part of his overall plan.

God has equipped you perfectly for his purpose. God knows your talents, your abilities, and even your flaws. He has orchestrated every aspect of your being to fit perfectly into his plan for your life and for the purpose he has for you. Trust in the importance you have in the eyes of your creator. One of the most important roles you have as a daughter to the King is to bring others to know who God is. You are to share that he sent Jesus to die on the cross for our sins so that through Him we may be saved. Bringing others to know Him is the most significant role anyone could possibly have, and God is entrusting that to you.

You Are Significant

Bible Reading

Jeremiah 1:5 Romans 8:28

Reflection

Are you ready to own your role as a Daughter of the King? Have you fully submitted in your relationship with God?

Not sure what your purpose is yet? That's okay! Think about what your abilities and talents are. What life experience have you had that can help others. Pray, read your bible, and repeat. Be still and listen. God will reveal his purpose to you and he will equip you to fulfill it.

Connection: Using Facebook or Instagram Share how God has shown your significance to his plan, share your testimony or an experience where God has specifically used you in the life of others.

Social Media: *You are significant! I am significant! #youare #sheperseveres*

Chapter Seven

You Are Strong

You Are Strong

Being strong can have different meanings as well as misconceptions. So, to clarify the strength we will be discussing is not physical but mental, emotional, and spiritual. The misconception of strength is that if you can get through difficult times, hardships, illness, or just life's ups and downs on your own you must be a strong person. However, true strength comes from not relying on yourself. You are not expected to do it all on your own. The strength you want to have, true strength, is when you completely die to self and submit yourself to Jesus. Letting go of your selfish desires, letting go of your fears, letting go of your worries, letting go of your ability to choose for yourself and letting go of yourself completely. This allows you to put all your needs and desires in God. Trusting Him enough to fully take over in all aspects of your life allows you to be the strongest you could ever be.

Asking for help is often viewed as a weakness. God's Word tells us we should cry out for his help and to fully trust Him. We should run to Him when we need a haven and find strength and rest in Him. He is our strength. We can do all things through Him which means we need Him to do all things, we cannot do them on our own.

On Wednesday, June 15, 2016, I was beyond surprised when I found out I was pregnant. I did the test on my own and wanted it to be a special surprise for my husband. He was out of town for work and would return home on that Friday so for two days I kept this huge and amazing surprise to myself. It was so hard for me to keep it a secret from Him we had found out together with every other baby. But that coming Sunday was Father's Day, so I thought it was perfect timing to wait and have a special gift for Him.

After revealing my surprise to my husband, we told our kids and the rest of the world via Facebook. I suspected I was around 4 -5 weeks pregnant when we found out. I was in baby planning mode once again and I was so excited. Unfortunately, my fear of losing the baby was at an all-time high. I couldn't explain the feeling I just had a deep gut-wrenching feeling that something was going to go wrong.

Then it happened on July 1, 2016, I started spotting. I knew right away I was losing the baby, but I tried my best to be positive. I went to the doctor and was told everything was fine. After a second trip to the doctor, the answers changed. At that second visit, I found out I was not only pregnant with one baby but with two, twins. Never in a million years would I have thought about having twins. I was completely taken aback.

The joy of having twins was instantly taken away as the doctor was unsure of the health of our babies. The doctor told me to be hopeful that it was possible I was just earlier in my pregnancy than expected. If that were true there was nothing to worry about. But I just knew, I knew my dates were correct and I knew I was losing my babies.

From that day on I cried every day pleading with God to save our babies even though in my heart I knew. I knew the babies were gone and I knew I was going to experience not only a miscarriage of one baby but a miscarriage of twins. I went back for another visit to confirm my fears I was miscarrying. I went home to try to miscarry naturally.

I grieved for so many different reasons for the loss of these babies than I did with the loss of Baby KW. I think because this pregnancy was so unexpected it made it sting just a little more since it ended so quickly. The fact that I was pregnant with twins means I lost two babies at the same time, I also lost an experience of raising twins. Losing the entire experience of having twins is a whole new feeling that is so hard to explain. I feel like having twins or multiples of any number is such a rare and special gift that it's like losing something you never knew you wanted and you will never get again. I hate when people assume a miscarriage is just a pregnancy that ended. I miscarried yes, but it discredits the loss so much, I had two babies growing inside of me and they died. My babies, my children died.

I also went through a different type of grieving period for these babies. I did not have to wait for an ultrasound to tell me my babies were gone, I already knew. I grieved for the loss of my babies before any medical professional told me they were gone. I spent weeks begging and pleading with God and literally hours crying out to Him. But then it hit me I knew they were already gone. I listened to the song "Thy Will" one night and at that moment, I let go of my own desires and just told God, "Okay this is it, I am surrendering to you and let your will be done, Thy Will Be Done". Even though it was something that completely broke me I knew I had to trust in his plan and have faith in Him. After weeks of waiting my body just was not letting the miscarriage complete naturally. I ended up having a D & C done which I really did not want to do just because I wanted to avoid surgery. Thankfully all went well with the surgery.

I knew I needed God to help me heal and simply face each day. It's during hardships we are often led directly to seek God's help through prayer. We should embrace his strength and seek his presence always but especially when we need his strength. By embracing our innate need for God's help especially during hard times we are exuding our true strength by acknowledging our need for help.

After months of seeking God for his love and his strength and trusting his plan for our family, he gave us another gift confirming our hope in Him. August 2017, I gave birth to a beautiful and healthy baby boy completing our family. Just like each of us, I know God has special plans for my sweet boy and I cannot wait to see how God uses Him. I could never have survived the loss of our babies on my own. It is a pain that never goes away, and I depend on God to get me through each day, each moment, and each painful memory. In God, I can be strong enough to move forward on my journey.

Remember that during our worst and hardest days God is never running from us he is always running directly to us to embrace us in his loving arms. We need to be vulnerable enough to seek Him for help, to be strong in Him. Show your true strength, reach out to God and allow Him to help you.

You Are Strong

Bible Reading

Romans 8:18 Ephesians 6:10

Reflection

What specific areas of your life can you seek God's strength for?

Is your pride hindering you from seeking God's strength? How can you let your pride go and be more vulnerable in seeking God?

Connection: Spend time focusing on the bible verses for this chapter. Be vulnerable with God in prayer and truly seek Him and focus on connecting with Him.

Social Media: *You are strong! I am strong! #youare #sheperseveres*

Chapter Eight

You Are Forgiven

You Are Forgiven

The term forgive is a verb as it is an action. When you forgive you are taking action to release any wrongdoing that may be bringing you hurt and resentment. Throughout the Bible, the concept of forgiveness is mentioned numerous times. The most significant act of forgiveness is, of course, Jesus dying on the cross for our sins. God sending his only son and Jesus willingly following his father plan to die for our sins to be erased was the ultimate act of love. Not only does the Bible teach of the forgiveness we have received through God's grace and Jesus's death, but we are also taught to forgive others. We should afford forgiveness to others as well as ourselves. It is important to understand regardless of popular opinion forgiveness also means forgetting.

For years I struggled with forgiveness. I could easily forgive those who wronged me. I could ask for forgiveness if needed. However, accepting forgiveness and forgetting my past was beyond difficult for me. I repented for my sins, for my past mistakes, past decisions, and I knew I was forgiven by God. However,

I couldn't accept the forgiveness and the guilt remained. I could not forgive myself for my past or forget it. I've learned that not forgiving myself is giving my past and my sins more power than Jesus dying on the cross. By not taking ownership of God's forgiveness I have allowed my past to affect all areas of my life. Including my relationship with my husband, my friendships, my education, my career, and my goals.

Focusing on the past keeps us from fulfilling God's plan for our present and our future. It could steal joy and blessings you will receive in the future. If you are worthy enough to God for Him to allow his own son to die for your sins and offer you forgiveness you are worthy enough to accept his forgiveness. You are worthy enough to forgive yourself and forget your past.

In Psalms 32:5 we are shown specifically not only does God forgive us of our sin when we repent but he also forgives the guilt we have because of our sins. "Then I acknowledged my sin to you and did not cover up my iniquity. I said, "I will confess my transgressions to the Lord." And you forgave the guilt of my sin. (NIV) After repenting our sins to God forgiving ourselves is so often easier than forgiving ourselves of the guilt our sins may carry. It makes forgetting our sins that much harder as well.

Have you found you are unable to forgive yourself because you first need to forgive someone else? It can be difficult to offer forgiveness when it has not been warranted. But that is exactly what grace is and who God calls us to be. We should strive to be a reflection of Jesus. This means offering grace to those who do not deserve it. By forgiving someone who has hurt you or wronged you in any way you will allow yourself to feel free from that burden and you can forgive yourself as well. You do not need to necessarily forgive them in person, but you need to offer true forgiveness. You could speak face to face, talk over the phone, send a text, communicate via social media, write a letter, or simply write a letter you do not intend to send just to release the forgiveness to them and therefore to yourself.

We need to accept God's forgiveness for ourselves otherwise we are being selfish and diminishing the power of Jesus's blood on the cross. By accepting God's forgiveness, we are robbing our sin and the enemy of having any power over us.

We should also forgive others. We are to be the reflection of Jesus. By forgiving others we are giving them what God has given us. It may be difficult to forgive others, but we always need to try to give others what God has given us not what others have given us. Don't allow Jesus' death to be in vain. We need to accept his forgiveness, forgive others, and forgive yourself.

You Are Forgiven

Bible Reading

Isaiah 43:18 Ephesians 4:32

Reflection

Take action! Forgive someone who has hurt you. How will you give your forgiveness; in person, mail a letter, write a letter that you do not intend to send?

Forgive yourself! Forgive your guilt and your shame! Write yourself a letter, in your journal, or in this book! Keep this letter as a reminder that you have forgiven yourself completely!

Connection: Let us know in our Facebook group that you have forgiven yourself and you have accepted Jesus' forgiveness!

Social Media: *You are forgiven! I am forgiven! #youare #sheperseveres*

Chapter Nine

You Are His

You Are His

Media and especially social media play a huge role in our lives today. I love social media! I enjoy sharing my journey as well as following others. Especially being able to keep up with family and friends as well as sharing our daily adventures is a joy. The problem with social media and media, as I previously mentioned is that it does not showcase our lives in everyday reality instead we showcase the reality we want others to perceive.

By trying to show only our best and intentionally perfectly created post we are drifting from sharing our authentic selves. We are viewing others perfectly presented lives via social media and that can leave us feeling envious and less than. As women confidence and self-worth can easily be damaged by comparing ourselves. This is especially true by means of the perceptions presented on social media and media such as television.

Recently our five-year-old little princess shared that she was struggling with her own confidence and self-esteem. As a momma to this (obviously perfect in my eyes) precious little girl I was beyond heartbroken. I did not understand where it was coming from. I make sure that I never speak negatively about myself especially not in front of my kids. We try our best to encourage and build each other up as a family. Our boys are always so sweet and remind their sister of how beautiful she is both inside and out. But she was still feeling less than and struggling with how others would think of her outer appearance. Absolutely heartbreaking, she is five years old, FIVE!

So, I wanted to share with you what I shared with my own little princess. In this media-crazed culture, it is so important to remember there is a difference between true reality and perceived reality. After discovering the source of her self-doubt (which was a television show about a specific blonde doll that even adult women compare themselves to) I was able to remind our princess of her true reality.

You are altogether beautiful, my love; there is no flaw in you.
Song of Solomon 4:7 (ESV)

This verse says it all. We were created by God. You were created by God. The same God that created this entire Universe. The same God that created the vast oceans. The same God that created the beautiful sunset behind the incredible mountainside. That same amazing God created you.

Instead of focusing on who you are, focus on whose you are! You are a princess because you are a daughter of the KING. You are a child of God. You belong to the Creator. Everything about who you are is derived from whose you are. Build your relationship with Jesus. Focus on God and the plans he has for you. The confidence you have should be in Him and his unending abilities that he will put to work through you. Your value and worth are immeasurable through Jesus. You are beautiful and flawless just as his Word says, therefore, stop comparing your reality to the perceived reality others are presenting.

Knowing you are a daughter of the King can not only give you a peaceful assurance in who you are it can also be overly intimidating. There can be a sense of responsibility to please God that can often overwhelm us. But as God's word tells us we are not to be afraid. Fear is the enemy's tactic to disconnect us from God. Instead, we should embrace being a daughter of the King and seek Him as our safe haven letting all intimidation, fear, and insecurities go.

Making God our priority and being intentional with the relationship we have with Him will alleviate the fears the enemy may try to impress on us. We must grow our faith in God and trust Him to fulfill all our needs as only he can. It's easy to become distracted by everyday life. We can try to fulfill our needs and our desires, yet it will never be enough. If we don't embrace who we are in Jesus and we are not intentional in cultivating a strong prioritized relationship with Him, we will never have enough. We will never have enough food, enough activities, enough clothes, enough money, enough relationships, enough intimacy, we will never have enough anything without God.

Our value is not measured in clothes, makeup, our homes, our cars, our education, our careers, or our bank accounts. Our value is measured in the relationship we have with Jesus and who we are in Him when we follow Him in faith and obey Him.

We need to embrace our role as a daughter of the King. As your relationship with Jesus begins to grow you may find Him asking you to do something out of your comfort zone. More times than not what God will call you to do will be inconvenient, uncomfortable, and nothing that you expect (me, right now, writing this book). When you step out in faith and obedience to do the hard thing you reflect the confidence you have God.

He created you perfectly for his plan and as Psalm 23:1 tells us you lack nothing! You will find peace in God you just need to allow Him to show you who he created you to be. Trust in who he is and what his plans for you are, Jeremiah tells us that his plans are for our success. Believe in what God has planned for you it is even more important than what you may see as most important in your life. As a daughter of the King, you need to keep your focus on whose you are.

You Are His
Bible Reading
Galatians 3:26 Romans 8:16

Reflection

How have you felt God asking you to step out in faith? How has that made you feel uncomfortable or unsure?

Knowing you are a daughter of the King how does that reassure you in moving forward in obedience of his calling?

Connection: Post a scripture on social media that relates to who you are in God and who he is calling you to be.

Social Media: *You are his! I am his! #youare #sheperseveres*

Chapter Ten

You Are You

You Are You

Something else we may have in common is if you have doubted yourself more times than not. Maybe you have felt like you are not who you are supposed to be. You're not doing what you're supposed to be doing. You are not living the life you're supposed to be living. I can tell you from personal experience if you are not living your life for God and you're not obeying his will for your life, you're right.

Don't fall for the enemy's tricks. His goal is to keep us far from God. If he has you focused on who you wish you could be then you are not focusing on who you already are in Jesus. The enemy wants to distract you from the purpose God already has in place for you.

If we are not living our lives for God and doing what he commands us to do, we cannot be who he created us to be. When we are not living out God's will for our lives we doubt not only ourselves but also the power of God that is within us. This creates the distance that leads to a disconnection from God that gives the enemy easier access into our lives. We need to put our focus on God and seek his will for our lives.

We need to remember that what we want for our lives and what God wants for our lives are two different things. Our desires wants, and dreams will usually not be the same as God's for our lives. We need to focus on God and understand his will for our lives and follow his will not our own. His way is the only way we will be completely fulfilled and live out our purpose.

Jesus calls Simon out in John 1:42 to not only give Him a new name but a new purpose. He says his new name should be Cephas which is translated to Peter. He is telling Simon that he is not living the life he should be living. He is telling Simon that he is not living his life as who he is supposed to be. He should be living his life for Jesus living as Peter. So, Jesus not only changes Peter's name he also renewed his life and fulfilled his purpose. Peter steps out in faith and obedience and owns who he is in Jesus. We need to be like Peter and step out without any fear in pure faith through obedience. This will allow Jesus to transform our lives as we live out our purpose through Him. God is our creator, he is the potter and we are the clay. We should not doubt who we are through Him. We should have faith in Him and his plan for us.

As Christian women, we have often heard of being a Proverbs 31 woman. If you have not read this scripture please do so now, Proverbs 31: 10-31. Okay, this woman is so not me, I mean come on she is perfect! As a tired mama to four children ages seven and under with a messy house and unending baskets of both dirty and clean laundry this woman is intimidating! I could never live up to her standard. If you read this scripture you may be like me and automatically start comparing yourself to her and start doubting who you are as a Christian, a wife, a mother, and just as a woman in general. Just like I previously discussed we must stop comparing ourselves to everyone's best day. We should trust in who God has created us to be on our best, worst, and every day in between.

I must share a little secret information that God recently revealed to me. Somehow every other time I have read or heard this scripture throughout my life I have missed this special little secret. Go back and read verse ten one more time. This verse tells us that this amazing and perfect woman who I could never live up to had servants! Wait, what? That's right ladies this woman had HELP! How I missed that little tidbit of valuable information every other time of my life is beyond me. But God including this information in verse ten is to me his way of reminding me and reminding you that we are not expected to be perfect. We are not expected to do things on our own. We are not expected to step out in faith and obedience on our own. We are expected to be ourselves. We are expected to have faith in Him. We are expected to obey Him. We are expected to trust Him. We are expected to make Him our priority. We are expected to fulfill his plan for our lives. We are expected to reach out to Him for help. We are expected to be his.

You are to fulfill God's greater purpose. God has never failed, and you have access to that same power through Him. When you establish an intimate relationship with Jesus and you live your life for Him he will help you and he will reveal his purpose for you. Fall in love with Him and who you are through Him. You are created perfectly for the purpose he has for you. You are created for his glory. You are created just the way you are for his greater plan.

You Are You
Bible Reading
Psalm 32:8 Proverbs 3:5-6

Reflection

Now that we have learned to trust God in defining who we are let's rewrite our new and truthful labels. Who are you now that you know whose you are?

Connection: Find our labels on our social media and share a name tag that fits you!

Social Media: *You are you! I am me! #youare #sheperseveres*

References

About The Author

Megan is a wife to her best friend and high school sweetheart, Jason. She is also a stay at home mom who homeschools their children. Megan has four children this side of Heaven with three more children awaiting them in Heaven. Megan and her family call Kentucky home while spending majority of their time on the road traveling. With a passion for writing, Jesus, and sharing her journey of loss and overcoming through faith Megan was inspired to share her journey to encourage others.

She Perseveres

Reminding women of their ability to overcome and persevere through God's unending grace.

Visit She Perseveres LLC and join a community of women just like you!

Find encouragement, inspiration, support, resources and join the journey to persevere.

Website: www.sheperseveres.com

Facebook:

https://www.facebook.com/sheperseveresllc/

Private Facebook Group: She Perseveres Group

https://www.facebook.com/groups/17265440807241
61/

Instagram:

https://www.instagram.com/sheperseveres/

Pinterest:

https://www.pinterest.com/sheperseveres/pins/

Pregnancy and Infant Loss

At the end of 2009 I suffered a missed miscarriage with our first child. Not only was I devastated by the loss but I was also lost myself. I did not receive any type of brochure, newsletter, packet, resources of any kind for my loss. Craving information and support I turned to the internet where I found I am not alone! One in four pregnancies end in miscarriage and statistics do not stop there as that does not include all the mothers who have lost their children due to ectopic pregnancy, stillborn, SIDS, and countless other heartbreaking stories.

In 2016 I experienced another devastating loss of our twins. Though we have been blessed with four healthy "rainbow" children the loss of our three babies is still very hurtful and a daily struggle. Not only do I want our three babies in Heaven to be remembered I also want to help others who have lost a child. I want to offer them my support, love, prayers, knowledge, and resources. I want others to know they are not alone and I want to raise awareness of pregnancy and infant loss. You can read my journey on my blog page.

The day I left the hospital after finding out we had lost Baby KW I left empty handed and the same as I left the doctor's office the following Monday. I was given no information about what missed miscarriage was, was their hope for me to have children in the future, no information for support groups, no information for memorial jewelry or ideas, no information about my rights at the hospital following the d and c, nothing. I feel like this is detrimental to the baby loss community. We should be supplying mothers, fathers, and families with all the great resources available to help them through this difficult journey.

Please go to
http://www.sheperseveres.com/resources/pregnancy-and-infant-loss/ for more information and resources.